# SELF CARE FOR THE WOUNDED SOUL

## 21 Days of Messy Grace

**Steve Austin**
with Kate Pieper, LMFT

# ALSO BY THE AUTHOR:

**From Pastor to a Psych Ward:**
**Recovery from a Suicide Attempt is Possible , 2016[1]**

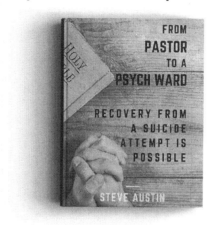

**The Writer's Toolkit:**
**How to Own and Craft Your Story , 2016[2]**

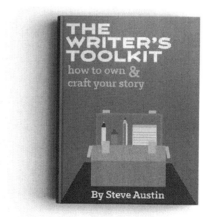

# DEDICATION

Self-care has saved my life and allowed me to thrive in a way I didn't even think was possible. If I had died four years ago I would've missed my wife becoming my best friend. I would've missed her laugh when I tell a really dumb joke. I would have missed that stuffed chicken she makes and the way she puts rose oil behind her ears after a bath. It smells so good. Most of all, I would've missed the amazing combination of strength and grace my wife has shown during my recovery.

I also would've missed the relationship I have built with my little boy. Ben Thomas turned one the day after I attempted suicide. I missed his first birthday, and I regret that. But I have loved every birthday since. Ben is my "joy boy"! Ben teaches me the wonder of childhood. He reminds me to let my imagination run wild. He is Steve Austin shrunk down into a 5-year-old frame. He's so much fun and adventure and stubbornness all rolled into one little package. If I had died four years ago, I would've missed getting to know the incredible little human being that he is.

It's still hard to believe, but if my suicide attempt had been successful, my daughter Caroline would not exist. Nothing smells as sweet as my little girl, fresh out of the bathtub. Her curly hair and her giant blue eyes light up the world. The gap between her two front teeth is about the cutest thing I've ever seen and it makes her a spitting image of her Mama. She is equal parts sweet and sassy. If I had died four years ago, Caroline never would have had the chance to make our family complete.

I've won awards to hang on the wall. I've had jobs with some really cool perks. I've interviewed famous people and had an essay or two gain widespread readership. But at the end of the day, the awards collect dust, jobs come and go, and famous people don't remember my name.

What matters?

The way Ben's eyes sparkle at 6am and 10pm, Caroline's little waddle as she runs to me at the end of a work day, and the way my wife still manages to look so beautiful when she's frazzled.

This book is dedicated to my family.

I'm the lucky one.

# FOREWORD
BY: KATE PIEPER, LMFT

I have had the privilege of working as a Licensed Marriage Family Therapist for some 20 plus years now. I am also a certified trauma therapist. I love working with people in the church who are walking through the confusion of depression, anxiety or abuse.

Helping others find freedom and healing is truly what God has designed me to do with my life.

However, I did not meet Steve Austin through my professional networking. I came across his refreshingly honest blogs about depression and anxiety on a very dark night for myself and my family.

A close family member had attempted suicide. My heart was breaking. And so, from the hospital emergency room - while waiting for transport for the family member to be taken to a psychiatric facility - I reached out to Steve. And Steve did what Steve does. He encouraged me and continued to check in on me and my family for the weeks afterwards.

Sometimes the church comes through the web, I guess!
I love Steve Austin. I love his ministry. I love his desire to embrace others in their mess and encourage them.

This testimonial Steve has written is a tool towards helping all of us embrace our mess. It is a practical tool with insight only someone who has "walked the walk" can write.

Thank you, Steve.

Thank you for the gift you are giving us by living wholeheartedly!

I trust you will be encouraged, as I am, by Steve Austin's practical and encouraging words. Steve is a voice we all need to hear for such a time as this.

Blessings to you as you walk this messy life with grace!

Kate Pieper, LMFT
**katepieperlmft.com**

# INTRODUCTION

When I was twenty-eight, I had a beautiful wife and a little boy who was almost a year old. I had a successful photography business and a career as a sign language interpreter. I had been serving in ministry for nearly a decade as a youth pastor and worship leader. From the outside, I seemed healthy and happy. But shame was choking the life out of me. I became convinced my only escape was suicide.

Why?

Partly because I was molested as a preschooler and secretly addicted to pornography for twenty years. I believed my life was pitiful and I was nothing but the sum of all my miserable mistakes and secrets. I'd spent hours, decades, begging God to change me at church altar calls.

But every time I stood up from the altar, I picked up that load of shame again and carried it right back out of the church. I was certain that in my inadequacy, I was beyond all hope and unworthy of love or belonging.

On September 20, 2012, I was finishing up an out-of-town assignment for work. That night I went back to my hotel room and ingested as much medication as I possibly could. Twelve hours later, I didn't show up for a shift. My clients became concerned and called the hotel. Hotel security soon discovered my body in a scene so gruesome they believed I had been murdered.

They called 911; I was rushed to the ER and transferred to the ICU. I eventually spent time in a psych ward for severe depression. The day I arrived in the ward was the day my life began to change.

Since that September day four years ago, I have been recovering from a suicide attempt, childhood sexual abuse, church hurts, and addiction.

I have learned that recovery is about digging. About finding. And about facing realities. It's been a long, hard process. But I have gained wisdom from leaning into my pain, in not allowing the hounds of hell to snap at my heels anymore. Now I turn around, call them by name, and let them know I am prepared to fight.

No more sweeping things under the rug. No more ignoring pain and hoping for the best. No more keeping up appearances. Recovery has forced me to peel back layers of shame and secrets and find the abundant life underneath.

Healing has come by learning it's actually healthy to consider my own feelings. To be compassionate to myself. To know my own limits. Because giving up is no longer an option.

There have been other struggles in the years since my suicide attempt. I haven't mastered this porn addiction completely, and I am not foolish enough to think there won't be other issues that crop up in the future. But after years of therapy, of practicing honesty and self-care, I know I can face whatever comes next.

Difficult times can only defeat me if I let them.

If you have ever felt hopeless, if you have ever believed that all the bad things in your life were beyond redemption, if you have ever felt unworthy of being loved or accepted, if you have ever feared what would happen if people found out whatever it is that haunts you - I get it.

I have been there, too. Maybe you are recovering from abuse, addiction, or a suicide attempt like me. Maybe you are struggling with anxiety or depression and don't know why yet. No matter what your starting point is, the tools in this journal will help you begin to answer the question, "Now what?"

You're tired of living this way.

You want to change your life, and you don't know where to begin.

I hope this journal will help you answer that question. It's time to take ownership of your life, and that begins with good self-care. It's hard work, but you can do it. No more running, no more hiding, no more masks. No matter what your journey has looked like so far, recovery is possible.

I am living proof.

# HOW TO GET THE MOST OUT OF THIS JOURNAL :

*First*, this book should in no way replace professional intervention, including (but not limited to) working with qualified mental health professionals and taking their recommended medications.

I am simply a man who has been there, offering my experience as a helping hand. Please do not ignore the advice of medical or mental health professionals. It could cost your life, and your life is much too valuable to take that chance. Trying to work through this in isolation can have devastating results. You need somebody invested in your care who can help see your blind spots.

*Second*, don't rush through it. This journey will lose all its meaning if you do. Take your time; recovery doesn't happen overnight. Make it your goal to read one section per day and focus on applying Kate Pieper's "Self-Care Reflections" at the end of each section.

*Third*, no one recovers in a vacuum. This journal is just a tool, only one piece of the recovery pie. We all need a real-life, flesh-and-blood support system to lock arms and walk down the road of healing with us. If you do not have one yet, please keep looking.

If you need somewhere to connect with others, the Grace is Messy: The Community Facebook group is a great place to start.

# DISCLAIMER

As in any book about abuse, there may be information in the material you are about to read that may "trigger" you in some way. Triggers can happen causing the following:

Flashbacks
Binge Eating
Drinking
Self-Harm
Depressed Mood / Anger
Irritability / Hopelessness

We are encouraging you to watch for any signs of "triggers" from this material. If you find yourself experiencing symptoms of having been "triggered," please do the following:

Deep breaths
Get centered by doing meditation and grounding
(HERE and NOW) exercises
Journal what the material is bringing up for you
regarding your past
Reach out for connection with someone safe

Finally, *this material is NOT therapy.* Steve Austin's story regarding his abuse, addiction, suicide attempt, and ongoing recovery is shared with the hope you will realize you too, can experience messy grace. You can recover and find encouragement through Steve's story. The self-care exercises are not a replacement for therapy or counseling. They are given as encouragement in the recovery process. The process of recovery is brave and beautiful.

We encourage you to pace yourself. We encourage you that if you find yourself "triggered" and unable to continue to read any day's material, give yourself grace and skip that paragraph or that day's reading . This is not a contest. There is no shame in taking a break for a day.

As always, we encourage professional support. If you need or want help in obtaining a therapist or a recovery group, please contact us. We will provide resources for you to locate a qualified therapist in your area.

– Steve and Kate

# TABLE OF CONTENTS

**DAY 14:** In the midst of anxiety, I will continue to look for beauty and goodness.

**DAY 15:** I will let go of what life should be like. Instead, I will accept circumstances as they are.

**DAY 16:** I get to choose who I let into my deep spaces.

**DAY 17:** If addiction is drowning, recovery is a life raft.

**DAY 18:** I will find my reason for getting out of bed each morning.

**DAY 19:** I will respect my limits, and focus only on things that make me better.

**DAY 20:** I don't have to live inside the identity of a person who was wronged forever.

**DAY 21:** I will be patient and kind with myself through the long-term process of recovery.

# DAY 1:
## I GIVE MYSELF SPACE TO BREATHE & JUST BE.

Four years ago, I was a youth pastor, sign language interpreter, wedding photographer, radio host, husband, and father. *In that order.* Long days and nights were the norm. I worked in a school full-time, had after-school activities, a radio show two nights a week, and church activities Wednesday night and all day Sunday. Even Saturdays were consumed with photoshoots and youth group activities. People wondered how I kept so many plates spinning. In my religious fervor and need to perform, I judged their lack of busyness as laziness.

My wife begged for attention. My friends constantly complained that I was missing in action. And my anxiety was through the roof. **I'd bought the lie that it was my job to save the whole world.** If not me, then who? Souls were at stake! Lives were hanging in the balance! How could I possibly sleep with the guilt of someone's eternal damnation on my hands?

Since the suicide attempt, I've learned the importance of personal space. I had no idea what I was missing, but my family certainly did. Now, instead of making major decisions without considering the impact on my family, I have made my wife and children my number one priority. As a result, I have started respecting their schedules and helping my wife balance duties at home. I've learned how important it is to unplug, to not live so focused on the next activity, to give myself time to just *be*.

These days, there's no radio show and no youth group. But I would be lying if I said I never feel the tug to do more. After all, busyness equals success, right? That lie was deeply ingrained, but all my busyness was just another way for me to hide. It helped propel me toward wanting to die. Self-care, I have learned, is more important than external success.

What is self-care? In a broad sense, experts define it this way:

*Self care includes any intentional actions you take to care for your physical, mental and emotional health. Good self care is a challenge for many people and it can be especially challenging for survivors of interpersonal violence and abuse. It can also be an important part of the healing process. Self care is unique for everyone.[3]*

For me, recovery and self-care are inextricably connected. My recovery from abuse, addiction, and a suicide attempt required dumptruck loads of self-care. In a nutshell, self-care often looks like giving myself grace. Grace: a word many people assume is reserved for Sunday morning. One that is sung in hymns and preached from the pulpit. And while grace certainly has its place in churches and cathedrals, grace is something every person is desperate for, if we're honest. Because at its root, grace is simply a second chance.

For me, it's been a second chance at a whole new life. For some people it's a second chance with a broken marriage or sobriety. No matter our pedigree, politics, or religious affiliation (if any), a second chance is something we all need sometimes.

My experience with recovery hasn't been a twelve-step program or long-term inpatient care. When I use the word "recovery," I am talking about healing. A journey toward wholeness. The entire journey is recovery. And that journey includes self-care and a whole bunch of grace.

From my personal experience, sometimes self-care means knowing that it's ok to have a good hard cry. Maybe it's closing your office door and taking some deep breaths. Or taking a "mental health day" because you just cannot push through another minute. Self-care is giving yourself permission to be first for a little while. It's not making excuses about why you can't do what you know in your gut you need to do. I'm a Christian, but I have found myself in a desperate place at times, needing something other than Jesus. Like a nap. And strong medicine. And a friend who will just listen.

Now I give myself space to rest and breathe. I start and end each day at the kitchen table with my wife and kids. We are more connected as a family than ever because I learned the hard way I do not need to be the savior of the whole damn world. We have less money, and fewer social plans, but that doesn't matter to me any more.

What does matter? My family. My health. Knowing who I really am. Now that I no longer pretend to have either a cape or a cross on my back, I can live out this wonderfully unpredictable and imperfect life I have been given as a gift to myself and the world. In letting go of the constant performance mindset of those who feel they must be saints, I realize that I am not loved by God *in spite of* who I am, but *because of* who I am.

Grace has changed my life. It will change yours too, if you let it.

**Self-Care Reflections:**

What is one thing you could quit today to give yourself some space to breathe?

_____

_____

_____

_____

_____

_____

_____

What activities feed your soul? Write them out.

_____

_____

_____

_____

_____

_____

Do you begin and end your day with self-care? If not,
what is one concrete step you can take toward that goal?

_____

_____

_____

_____

_____

_____

_____

## Messy Grace Mantra:

I don't have to have it together all of the time, or even some of
the time. I can take time to care for myself.

# DAY 2:
## I AM TAKING OFF THE MASK.

For years, I believed I would never truly belong anywhere if people knew the real issues I faced on a daily basis. I did my best to cover up my struggles by performing in all areas of life. I even put on an act for my wife and in my faith community.

It worked great for a while.

Until it all came crashing down.

When I woke up in ICU and saw the expressions of my wife and her best friend, I knew the show was over. They had seen the less-than-impressive little man behind the curtain.

When it was time to head home, my stomach dropped at the thought of facing anyone I knew. For years, I thought life came with two choices: act like a normal person, or let everyone see I was "crazy." Now everyone knew I'd been *acting* for decades. I wanted to get back to "normal," but I wasn't even sure what normal was any more. I wanted to stop being a fearful fraud, to become confident, but how?

My wife and I decided if we were going to stay together, we'd have to see a therapist. It was one of the best decisions we could have made. Therapy saved our marriage and my life, but it required me to admit I wasn't okay. People thought our individual lives and our marriage were perfect, but we were isolated and afraid under that mask. I wouldn't go back to that place for anything.

Therapy taught us to allow our honest brokenness to draw us together. We had never wrestled with our emotions before, but now Lindsey and I discuss hard stuff and work through our doubts and insecurities. As we dig things up, we talk about them because we are determined to be honest. We no longer perform for others or each other.

Early in my recovery, I didn't want my extended family or friends to know about my suicide attempt, and I certainly didn't want to face the local church. It had been my home for nearly three decades and I had often been the star of the show. I'd been a performer in every sense of the word. After such a massive personal failure, I wasn't sure I fit in anyone's church anymore.

The church still freaks me out, yet I refuse to disengage. Being surrounded by those who knew the old me still feels like a lot of pressure. I show up anyway. Because disengaging is no longer an option. I am determined to live what Brene' Brown refers to as a wholehearted life, and sometimes that means doing the harder thing. It also means no longer being obsessed with the opinions of other religious people, but staying rooted in what God thinks of me.

Refusing to fake it means I don't laugh at every forced joke from the pulpit, just to fit in. And sometimes I don't even go. It also means not faking it in relationships. I used to believe I was supposed to be friends with everyone.

Today, I have four close friends, not counting my wife. But I have lots of acquaintances. People who I don't owe anything other than decency and politeness. In the words of my friend Sue (one of those four friends), "They aren't sleeping with me and they aren't coming to my funeral, so their opinion doesn't count." I don't live my life, based on the opinions or approval of acquaintances any longer.

These days, my faith is still a very large part of my life, but a flesh-and-blood support system is equally important, plus excellent self-care which includes: diet, exercise, and prescribed drugs. Finding this balance has made me the healthiest version of myself I have ever been.

**Self-Care Reflections:**

Are you wearing a mask for the sake of others or for self-preservation? If so, what is it?

_____
_____
_____
_____
_____
_____

This week, identify one struggle. Maybe it's a past hurt, bad theology that damaged your view of God, or something else. Name it.

_____
_____
_____
_____
_____
_____

This entire journal is about learning to take off the mask. How will you be kind to yourself as you consider changing your life?

_____
_____
_____
_____
_____
_____

## Messy Grace Mantra:

Taking off the mask begins with saying I am not okay. I will be honest with myself.

# DAY 3:
## I DESERVE SAFETY, LOVE, & BELONGING.

Early in recovery, my biggest struggle was getting past my own sense of inadequacy. I believed I wasn't man enough, husband enough, father enough, Christian enough, and certainly not sane enough to meet the expectations of those around me. It seemed like "normal" people were learning what a phony I'd been, and I feared I would never be loved or accepted again.

Shame clouds our judgment, preventing us from seeing our own self-worth. It's hard to see the value you bring to the world when you hate yourself.

In the beginning of my time on the psych ward, the experience felt silly. It appeared that we were focusing on basic things, like eating right, getting plenty of rest, and sharing our problems. In retrospect, I see that what we were doing was much deeper. We were engaging in a community of people with similar struggles and similar goals, we were setting boundaries, and we were learning about self-compassion.

In one particular community session, the counselor taught that when emotions go up, rational thinking goes down. This statement rang true. It was part of my problem. In the past, when the really bad days showed up, I would engage anyone willing to listen. I was looking for any opportunity to talk about past hurts. I wanted someone to validate my pain, but I wasn't really interested in getting to the root cause of my issues. I would vent, shout, and cry, but failed to seek practical steps to work through my problems.

After I was released from the hospital, I immediately found a counselor. Having a professional, unbiased third party, who is paid to tell you the truth as they see it, is a powerful medicine. In therapy, I was still able to vent, shout, and cry, but I was also given homework, similar to what you are doing in this self-care journal.

Recovery takes time. You'll pass through some parts quickly, and some you'll need to go back and repeat. This book isn't designed to heal you. It's designed to empower you to start the process. This is just beginning.

In the safety of the hospital community, I also learned the value of self-compassion. Folks with mental illness tend to be extremely compassionate toward others, but we often do not show ourselves the same grace. But self-compassion is absolutely necessary to have a whole, healthy life. We must be kind to others, and we must also be kind to ourselves. As a part of my recovery, I am working through Brene' Brown's teachings[4], learning to speak to myself the same way I would speak to someone I love. It is making a big difference in healing my own shame.

Self-compassion sometimes looks like being kind to yourself when you screw up. And in recovery, you will screw up. Recovery is not always easy. Relapse is common. The important thing is to be kind to yourself and get back up and try again.

**Self-Care Reflections:**

> Over the next twenty-four hours, write three compliments for yourself in the space provided.

Where do you see the effects of shame in your life?

_____
_____
_____
_____
_____
_____

We're usually kinder to others than we are to ourselves. Think of a recent failure and imagine a loved one experienced it instead of you. How would you extend grace and encourage them?

_____
_____
_____
_____
_____
_____

## Messy Grace Mantra:

I will speak kindly to myself. I will practice treating myself as I would want my best friend to be treated.

# DAY 4:
## I WILL FIND HEALING, NOT JUST ESCAPE.

When I was 12, I discovered porn. What started as teenage curiosity turned to fascination, and eventually a powerful addiction. For nearly ten years of my addiction, I was a youth pastor in the Bible Belt.

I was covered in shame. When sexual abuse is your first conscious memory, an over-sexualized life is pretty common, but I didn't know that at the time. I thought something was wrong with me. I begged God to heal me, and as a teenager I confessed to a youth leader. Over and over, he prayed and believed for the blood of Jesus to heal me. But no one ever offered any practical steps to teach me how to walk away from a powerful addiction.

Often in Christian circles, there's room for recovering alcoholics and drug addicts, but most church people don't know how to discuss porn addiction. There's no freedom for any Christian – much less a pastor – to say, "my drug of choice is porn." Throughout my teenage years and early twenties, I overcompensated for my insecurities by masking my pain with humour and good behavior. I lived in constant fear of my perfect image being shattered with the truth.

Just as terrifying was the fear my wife would eventually tire of my struggle, and decide I was not enough. I was certain if she really knew me, she would leave me. It sounds irrational now, but I would have rather died than face my shame.

The day our marriage counselor connected the dots between my abuse, addiction, and suicide attempt changed my life. She helped us see the common thread through the whole story: shame. If I was going to get better, I was going to have to deal with my shame.

Addiction of any kind thrives in isolation. It takes you somewhere you never intended to go. The secrecy pulls you away from safety, away from community, and away from true intimacy. In addiction, there are two battles: breaking free and staying free. Breaking free starts with a single moment of vulnerability, but staying free requires much more.

I learned how to stop escaping and began finding actual healing from my addiction by understanding:

> The stresses, places, and moments that push me into my addictive behavior.
> Knowing what to do instead, in the moments of stress and isolation.
> Instead of condemning myself when I fall, I am learning to celebrate every victory, even small ones. I am committed to creating a new future for my family.

I am gaining more tools, strength, and support each day. I want to be the man my wife and children deserve, so I am taking active steps down this road to recovery. And that path is paved, brick by brick, with intentional steps of vulnerability, honesty, and courage.

**Self-Care Reflections:**

> What is one way you can speak back to shame when it shows up?

_____
_____
_____
_____
_____
_____
_____

Addiction thrives in isolation. One way to defeat it is to have an escape plan. For me, I know there are days I don't need to be home alone. I know I don't need to stay up late at night on the computer, long after everyone else has gone to bed. What is your escape plan?

_____

_____

_____

_____

_____

_____

_____

## Messy Grace Mantra:
I will feed my soul. I will look for healing and not just escape.

# DAY 5:
## GOD HEALS ORDINARILY.

Abuse comes in many forms. There are red marks and red eyes, but what about the deep wounds? Nobody sees those.

For the longest time, I wondered why nobody intervened. Why did no one come to my rescue in the dusky glow that summer evening? Where the hell was my Mama? And where was Jesus in that moment? Why didn't he stop it? We all wish for that, don't we? Unfortunately, bad things happen. There's no getting around that. We all wish for a magical way to avoid or skip over the hardest moments of our lives, but that hardly ever happens.

We all wish for a miraculous way out of our circumstances. If we're Christians, we expect God to come through, to swoop in and save us from ourselves. We want Super Jesus to show up on our balcony, cape flapping in the wind. But the truth is, Jesus doesn't typically save you from yourself.

Instead, God healed me ordinarily: through intense therapy, marriage counseling, lots of reading, and anxiety medication. Sure, God can magically fix your problems. But usually he doesn't. He works through friendships, marriages, Sacraments, church community, medication, and qualified professionals.

In the finding, in the daily working-out of salvation, there is both a cleansing and a cleaving. Cleaving to the only Hope that has ever pushed me to face those demons head-on and helped me survive when I did it. Cleansing in every private moment I have with the only One who backs up His promise to never leave me alone.

**You just keep digging.**

You dig down deep and find the root of the pain. Once you have found it, you keep digging until you can find grace to keep going.

The world is a cruel place, and we're all looking for kindness. For grace. And grace found me in a hospital bed, longing to die. I was literally at the end of my rope, but grace looked like a second chance from my wife and professionals who urged me to acknowledge my trauma as part of the healing process. I began to lean into my pain and eventually, I was able to wake up and stand up and say, " *Everything about this was wrong".*

In my experience, grace looked like the person of Jesus, I had always read about in the Bible. He came alongside me: the outcast, the reprobate, the loser. The grace of God was with me in the midst of the most painful parts of recovery. Where religion would have abandoned me, caught in the red tape of legalism and rules I could never fully follow, Jesus refused to leave me.

God remains faithful and present, even in the midst of our darkest tragedies. But he never allowed my pain to be cheapened by sweeping it under the rug in front of the altar. Instead of snapping his fingers and healing me in an instant, he has allowed me to name my pain and has walked through the broken places with me. God has shown me that he is present in the process. I am still uncomfortable with other men, my own peers or in intimate settings, but Jesus lingers with me as he gently restores my soul. And that is a miracle.

**Self-Care Reflections:**

In his book, *Lion and Lamb: The Relentless Tenderness of Jesus*[5], Brennan Manning says, "Healing our image of God heals our image of ourselves." How do you see God? Is God a celestial taskmaster who demands perfection? Is God aloof and uninvolved in the mess of your life? Is God a patient, gracious, compassionate parent who is intimately involved in the details of your life and refuses to let you walk through recovery alone?

_____

_____

_____

_____

_____

_____

If you are a little further along in the recovery process, in what ways have you experienced the ordinary ways God heals us?

_____

_____

_____

_____

_____

_____

In the last section, you were encouraged to write a letter. Now that you have named your pain, will you name your expectations? What do you want to get out of this? In what ways are you longing for healing? Where would you like to become more whole?

_____

_____

_____

_____

_____

_____

_____

## Messy Grace Mantra:

I will remember a loving and compassionate God is the one who is doing the work inside of me. I will believe He is faithful to bring it into completion.

# DAY 6:
## SHAME NO LONGER GETS A VOTE IN MY LIFE.

Nothing made sense. I saw flashes of light, heard incoherent chatter. I had done everything I could to make sure I never woke up again. *Why am I here?!* I'd been overwhelmed with life and the way things seemed to be crumbling around me. *I just wanted to die.*

A nurse with scissors sliced through my clothes. The force of shame punched me in the gut as cool air hit my bare skin. Strangers lifted me onto a hospital bed. *Why are they touching me?!* It's just a flash of memory. In the next moment I was out again, but in that semi-conscious space, I remember only shame. I wasn't ashamed of trying to kill myself. I was ashamed of being seen.

I was barely alive, but knowing strangers could see my body still tapped into the deep humiliation of childhood abuse. It was nothing new; my whole life was marked by shame and fear. I was scared of so much. I was afraid someone would discover my addiction, afraid I would turn into a perpetrator, afraid I would cheat on my wife, afraid of what would happen if people knew about that little white pill I took every day because I was so loaded down with fear and anxiety. I've since learned a life marked by fear is common for victims of childhood sexual assault. But back then all I knew was I'd rather die than continue to live with the constant fear and shame.

For years, I tried to find healing at altar calls and prayer benches. Shame told me I could never be honest about my struggles. So I tried to clean myself up, live up to unrealistic expectations of religious people, and never let them see my real issues. I thought if I just prayed hard enough, God would love me. If God would just love me enough, He could work a miracle in my life, and this would all be over.

I was so wrong.

It makes some people uncomfortable, but the truth is, God's perfect love wasn't enough to heal me. No matter how hard the traveling evangelists preached or prayed at my Grandma's country church, Jesus wasn't snapping His fingers and fixing this mess. It took practical, real life steps. For me, healing came from honesty, medication, therapy, and from doing the hard work.

Yes, God was involved every step of the way, but it didn't happen at an altar. And it didn't happen magically or overnight. The healing is still happening. I've learned to trust God to lead me through this process. As he reveals another layer of pain or shows me that I've been responding to my trauma in unhealthy ways, he invites me to enter into the healing.

I didn't just receive compassion from Jesus, but from my wife. When I had given up on myself, Lindsey's trust in God's goodness was unwavering. And her faith in me was just as stubborn. Others didn't understand why she stayed, but she trusted the man she knew I was under all those layers of shame and mess. I wanted to wall myself in and keep trying to hide, but Lindsey climbed down into the muck with me and refused to let me go.

It wasn't easy. Wading through this kind of heaviness never is. But as long as I continued to be truthful, she was willing to help me tear down walls that had kept us apart for years. Because Lindsey was willing to stick with me through the worst imaginable moments, my life is more open and hopeful than I ever dreamed it could be.

According to Brene' Brown, "Shame cannot survive being spoken."[6] I hid the abuse for so long that my unintentional habit is still to hide. My gut response is to escape. Still, I continue to push myself to be open and honest with safe people and create practical boundaries. I intentionally loosen the grip of shame on my life every day, a little at a time. For me, for my wife, and for our children.

But I do have boundaries. They are vital. Brene' Brown also says, "You respect my boundaries, and when you're not clear about what's okay and not okay, you ask. You're willing to say no."[7] And she's right. People who think they are being courageous by airing their dirty laundry to anyone who will listen aren't being vulnerable, they are being unwise. In recovery, you have to know who is trustworthy and who isn't. And trust me, not everyone can be trusted.

When buried memories begin bubbling up, the worst thing we can do is shove them back down and close the lid. All that pain has a way of seeping back to the surface. It might take months or even decades, but in time it will always ooze out.

So what do you do?

Take a step toward deliberate "safe relationships" with people who will not shame you through this process or gossip about your recovery. And take a step away from hiding and performance. I tried to keep up appearances for thirty years and it nearly killed me. Don't let it kill you.

**Self-Care Reflections:**

> Maybe you're not ready to tell your shame story to someone else just yet. But can you begin thinking about what your truth might be?

_____

_____

_____

_____

_____

_____

_____

Who are the people in your life who you can trust? How would your relationships with them look different if you began to share your truth with them?

_____
_____
_____
_____
_____
_____
_____

List people you know are not safe to share your story with. While it is important to walk out of shame and secrecy, it is also important to cherish the healing process by recognizing that some people will not be invited on this journey.

_____
_____
_____
_____
_____
_____
_____

## Messy Grace Mantra:

God is present with me through this journey and will either save me from the darkness and heaviness of shame or walk through it with me.

# DAY 7: I AM ALIVE. I WILL NOT FORGET HOW IMPORTANT THAT IS.

Even before I tried to kill myself, *I wasn't living.* I had hurts and fears and bitterness and resentment and mess that nearly killed me. I have said it countless times: *there is no medical reason for me to be here. But I am.* And it is only because of the goodness of God.

His grace is so much greater than our wildest imaginations. He let me find a life I didn't even know I could have. A wholehearted life is so much deeper than just inhaling and exhaling. This extraordinary God shows up in a thousand ordinary moments and shows me what that life looks like.

Growing up, I heard people say, "The eyes are the window to the soul." Before my suicide attempt, my eyes weren't empty. They were just forgetful. I'd forgotten to look for the good things in life. But now, I am finding joy in the most mundane places: at the kitchen table with my wife, working through deep-seated fears; in every intentional moment I spend with my children, cultivating their innocence and self-worth; and even on the couch at the counselor's office.

I am happy now. That did not seem possible before.

Remembering to look for good in people and situations is hard, but it helps. Celebrate the gracious people God brought alongside you in the journey. For me, the nurse who cared for me while I was in ICU sticks out as a real guardian angel. Plus there are friends I never expected to support me in my recovery, but do. Life sucks at times, but when we find things to celebrate, we shouldn't just gloss over them.

*I'm alive.*

There are plenty of reasons to celebrate, but the fact that I didn't die is reason enough for me. I don't want to forget that.

**Self-Care Reflections:**

What do you enjoy? Is it the smell of fresh cut grass? The taste of soda through a straw? Notice the details of your life that are pleasant, even fun. Make a note to notice something every day. Write them down when you can and give yourself something to look back on.

_____

_____

_____

_____

_____

_____

Do you have a person you're especially thankful for? Tell them today. And tell them why.

_____

_____

_____

_____

_____

_____

According to Kate Pieper, LMFT, studies show the brains of depressed people often do not even see the bright colors of the world they live in. All of life is shrouded in the darkness of depression. So today's challenge is to get outside and notice bright and vibrant color. Write them down. Is it the richness of a wildflower? The blue of the sky? The green of the grass underneath your feet? Or the stark white of the clouds, contrasting behind the trees? Whatever it is, take time to notice and really see the world we live in.

---

---

---

---

---

---

---

## Messy Grace Mantra:
I am grateful for my breath and grateful I am ALIVE!

# DAY 8:
## I AM MORE THAN MY DIAGNOSIS.

I will never forget meeting the psychiatrist before I was transferred from ICU to the psych ward. I was nervous as he entered the room, clipboard in hand. He gave me my diagnosis, then gave a brief overview of what to expect in the coming weeks. But I didn't hear his plan. All I could think was, *I'm now officially crazy.* My palms were sweaty, my breathing shallow, as I remembered my Aunt Missy, who killed herself when I was a teenager. I remembered the way people whispered about her when she was alive, both around town and in our family. I feared life would be exactly the same for me.

I was convinced a diagnosis meant I would never be able to find a respectable job. My kids would have to grow up with their friends talking about their crazy dad. Everyone would think I heard voices and belonged in a padded room. It made me feel less than a real human. I believed I would never find full acceptance in any community again. Except, of course, with other mentally ill people. As the doctor's voice droned in the background, I stared out the window, wishing for any kind of escape.

The stigma of mental illness sucks. But not getting better sucks worse. Those of us with a diagnosed mental illness just want our lives back. We want to get better. For me, one of the biggest hurdles was learning to focus on getting better, instead of the label.

Labels are important, especially from a medical standpoint. They give us a plan of action. They show us a lot about our limits. They teach us which medications may help and what substances or situations to stay away from. But when we focus more on the label than the person behind it, a human being in need of love and belonging, we miss the point. And we miss an opportunity to live a full and meaningful life.

In the psych ward, I learned I needed to define my triggers: those things that cause my anxiety to increase or my depression to worsen. For me, it's as simple as black coffee and as complex as not spending days alone at a time. (Isolation can be a real son of a bitch for someone with a mental illness).

I had to create a plan I could follow. My short-term strategy included intense therapy with professional counselors, psychologists, and psychiatrists during the first couple of years of my recovery. Eventually, the intensity tapered off, but I know I can still make an appointment any time. My plan also included medication, which was much stronger in the beginning than it is now. The truth is, I will always take medication of some type.

When depression and anxiety descend like a fog, following the doctor's prescribed dose of medication often clears the sky so I can find myself again. It makes me more of who I am, not less.

Another part of my plan was to name my support system, the people I can lean on in hard times, the ones who could handle my needs. In the four years since my recovery, I have experienced various reactions from people. Some can handle the recovery process. Some aren't at a place where they can handle it. Some friendships are seasonal and some are for a lifetime. During recovery, I think you should expect people to come and go from your life. And that's ok.

Each segment of my recovery plan has carried me a step further down the road to healing.

While I have learned to accept my diagnosis, it doesn't define me. It gives me boundaries and forces me to embrace self-care. I have depression and anxiety, but it doesn't get to determine who I am. I am much more than a label or the stigma attached to it.

**Self-Care Reflections:**

Begin creating a plan, similar to the one above. Keep it as simple as listing practical self-care, your support system, helping professionals and making a list of your medications. You can do that in the space provided.

_____
_____
_____
_____
_____
_____
_____

Who could make up your support system? Has yours, like mine, changed over time?

_____
_____
_____
_____
_____
_____
_____

Has a professional given you a diagnosis? How has that affected you? How does the diagnosis feel? How are you processing it?

_____
_____
_____
_____
_____
_____
_____

## Messy Grace Mantra:

**I am not my diagnosis.**

I am _____ (state your name)
and I am a _____ (insert a positive trait),
_____ (insert another positive trait),
_____ (insert one more positive trait)
who is growing and becoming every day.

Below is additional space to write out positive declarations, affirmations, and encouragements for yourself and your future.

_____
_____
_____
_____
_____
_____
_____
_____
_____
_____
_____
_____
_____
_____
_____

# DAY 9:
## I WILL NOT IGNORE MY SYMPTOMS.

It's easy to try and write off my symptoms. I can call it stress or just a case of the blues, but if I leave them untreated for too long, they scream for attention with a full-blown panic attack.

Culture tells us to shake off our bad days and ignore telltale signs of mental health issues. But if I had cancer, I might listen to a naturopath's advice to drink special juices, cut out refined sugars, or follow the path of meditation to wholeness.

*But I would still take chemo.*

Mental illness is a real thing. A disease. When the doctor says the chemicals in your brain aren't firing properly and a certain medication will help level you out, listen to the doctor. Sweet older women think they're being encouraging when they talk about the freedom that Jesus can bring, so you won't be dependent on medication. But that just causes shame to simmer and reinforce the urge to ignore warning signs.

It took a few tries to find the meds that were right for me. Some made me too sleepy, some made me too grumpy, but eventually we settled on meds that helped me find my new normal. In the end, it was worth the hassle.

Another thing I've learned is not to rely on my primary care physician to help me sort out the complicated maze of mental health. I'm not a professional, but you wouldn't go to your family doctor for cancer treatment. So why would you do that for psychiatric needs? There's no shame in seeing a specialist to work out the best course of treatment. A therapist who has experience in understanding the effects of medication can help you quarterback the effectiveness of the medicine and communicate with your psychiatrist.

Counseling was another important part of my recovery. After my suicide attempt, spending time with a professional ultimately saved my life. I learned many things during the intense first few months of counseling, but what stands out most is that issues in my marriage centered around a lack of trust and an abundance of shame. The moment the therapist helped connect all my dots back to the day I was molested, nearly thirty years before my suicide attempt, my whole world changed. When I was able to put a name to my overwhelming emotion, to begin studying shame and the effects it had on every area of my life, I began to heal.

That healing is still happening. Good doctors and therapists have taught me to pay attention to my warning signs. The medication I take for my symptoms ensures I stay healthy enough to continue that healing process, because recovery is a lifelong journey.

**Self-Care Reflections:**

List some symptoms you have emotionally and physically as part of your recovery process. Which ones are the most difficult to admit?

_____

_____

_____

_____

_____

_____

_____

What are some practical ways you are dealing with your symptoms? (this includes medication)

_____

_____

_____

_____

_____

_____

_____

Are there support groups or people in your area you can connect with who are grace-oriented? Please list these groups. What are the pros and cons of attending?

_____

_____

_____

_____

_____

_____

_____

## Messy Grace Mantra:

I deserve healthy support from myself and grace-filled people.

# DAY 10: TODAY WILL NOT LAST FOREVER. HARD DAYS DON'T DEFINE MY LIFE.

Even thirty years after the fact, I still struggle with the ripple effects of being abused. When I walk into a public restroom, I am a nervous wreck. I scan the area without being aware that I'm doing it. I have to know who is there, who is with me, who could be watching me. And I never use the urinal.

When I stand in the stall with the door locked (I won't use one without a lock) and someone goes in the stall next to me, I hear the little metal lock latch on their stall. That freaks me out, too. I immediately look behind me to see if someone is standing there.

I'm not a child any more, but in those moments, I certainly feel like one.

While no one is ever walking in, in my mind someone is *always* there. I hate that my abuser still has so much power over me. Yet that's not true. It's not him, it's the memory of him. And sometimes our memories are a prison, even though we walk around like we're free. We go to work, to church, to play, while these prison bars stare us down, constantly reminding us of the trauma we carry with us.

The bathroom smells like sweat mixed with urine. It smells unclean, dirty, dank: words that make my skin crawl. It's the same smell from that summer evening in Alabama, in the side yard beneath the shadow of the pink crêpe myrtle.

This is where grace gets messy. It's the part nobody wants to share. In the bathroom stall, I hold on to joy when hell is screaming in my ear. It's the kind of mercy no one ever wants, but so many of us need.

Maybe it's not the memory of abuse for you. Maybe it's the loss of your child. Or maybe you found the body of a loved one who left this world of their own choosing. Whatever your story, trauma is miserable.

It creates a graveyard in our memory and drags us through it under the shadow of a hulking moon.

I have a four-year-old little boy who made it, unscathed, through the year my life changed forever. When I see just how normal he is, my celebration is mixed with grief. I celebrate how wonderful and wild and funny and smart and brilliant and innocent he is. And I mourn the little boy I never got to be. I've been looking over my shoulder for thirty-three years. I've never felt as carefree as he does. Yet of course, I'm so thankful that my boy will never know the fear, anger, and confusion I have experienced for most of my life.

My son is part of my redemption. But as sweet as redemption may taste, I fear I'll always be that preschooler when I'm in a public restroom.

I don't like bad days or flashbacks. *Who does?* I hate when mental illness seems to get the best of me. I hate the semi-permanent knot in my throat, avoiding eye contact with co-workers, the constant urge to run home. I hate the voice of shame that whispers, *"What a loser. Get your shit together. What's wrong with you?"* I hate the lies that tell me I wouldn't struggle if I just had more faith.

The power of a second chance has changed my life. **Maybe the most important thing to remember is that a flashback is not a setback.** I'm thankful that flashbacks aren't real. Most often, they are the darkest, scariest portions of our trauma. They are unpredictable and unfair, but I choose to keep living. Rather than allow the fear of the next flashback to hold me captive, I am choosing to embrace truly good parts of life, especially when anxiety tries to overwhelm me. Come what may, life goes on.

If this is all new to you, remember to take hard days one day at a time. Hard days don't last forever. For me, sometimes hard days mean I take an extra five minutes on a lunch break to hide in the server room at work and take a few deep breaths. If necessary, I am also not afraid to take medicine my doctor has prescribed specifically for those moments, or even take a "mental health day." I'm not an advocate of hiding under the covers, but I also believe in knowing yourself well enough to acknowledge your limits. If the day is bad enough and you don't put your job in jeopardy, there is nothing wrong with saying, "I will try again tomorrow."

**Self-Care Reflections:**

How do you currently handle a hard day?

What can you do differently when a hard day is kicking your butt?

Where do you find inspiration on especially hard days? (Examples: music, poetry, photos, etc.)

## Messy Grace Mantra:

I will be patient with myself and this process. God is setting the pace of my healing as I join with Him.

# DAY 11: I DON'T OWE ANYONE AN APOLOGY FOR MY STORY.

When others don't understand mental illness, they can make comments that seem to have a hidden meaning. Sometimes it's intentional and sometimes it's just plain ignorance. Either way, those jabs bring on shame. If I feel like someone thinks I should have my life more together than I actually do, I feel a need to say I'm sorry.

But I don't owe anyone an apology for my recovery. I don't have to feel bad for having a hard day. And I definitely don't need to say ask forgiveness for having a panic attack.

In my book, *From Pastor to Psych Ward*, I talked about the time during my little boy's toddler days when it seemed he was sick all the time. He would often vomit and make major messes. Each time, he would cry, but not because he didn't feel good. "Dada," he would say, "I'm sorry I frowed up." It broke my heart.

The truth is, my son couldn't control his stomach trouble any more than I can control my panic attacks. Both are inconvenient and problematic, but I wouldn't choose to have a meltdown in the middle of my office any more than someone would willingly choose to throw up in the middle of the living room floor.

I want people to know it's okay to have a meltdown. I've found myself in desperate times and places where I needed something other than Jesus. Like a nap. Strong medicine. A good, hard cry. Or a friend who will just listen.

My life changed when I started letting others' opinions go. My wife's family doesn't like me, trust me, or believe in me. Not one single in-law is supportive. And for a few years after the suicide attempt, it really bothered me. Does it still hurt? *Sure, it does.* But I no longer allow their opinions to control me. I am fully aware of the mistakes I've made, but I have moved on.

My life is nothing like it was before the suici`de attempt. I am a new person. I choose to live today, instead of carrying around the shame of my past.

Not everyone in the world is kind. Not everyone follows the *Golden Rule* or holds back harsh opinions. Not everyone has your best interest in mind. The fact remains that some people are jerks and there's nothing you can do about it.

I also had to let go of others' thoughts about telling my story. It bothered friends and family on both sides when I went public. But lives are changed by stories. And learning to own my recovery was an integral part of my healing. I don't owe anyone an apology for my mental illness or my story. You don't either.

**Self-Care Reflections:**

If you're given the opportunity to apologize for your struggles or diagnosis this week, I dare you not to.

_____

_____

_____

_____

_____

_____

_____

Whose opinion hurts the most? Can you tell them? If not, what is one step you can take today to move past it and allow yourself to live your own life for yourself?

_____

_____

_____

_____

_____

_____

_____

What is one go-to phrase you can use regarding your limitations when others ask about them? For instance, instead of, "Thanks for the invite to the party, I just really don't do well in crowds currently." You could say, "Thank you, but I will have to pass this time."

_____

_____

_____

_____

_____

_____

## Messy Grace Mantra:
I will remember that other people's opinions are none of my business.

# DAY 12: MY FAILURES DO NOT DEFINE MY CHARACTER OR MY WORTH.

No one likes to make mistakes, but even worse, nobody wants their shortcomings to be public. In the age of social media and blogs, we all experience the concept of living in a fishbowl now more than ever. **The thing is, most folks don't know enough about fish until the fish is floating to the top.**

I've never seen this struggle more than during my years in traditional ministry. When you are a pastor, everything you do has the potential of being scrutinized by everyone you know. There are those who want to hold you accountable and there are those who long to see you (and the Church universal) crumble. I remember the nights of driving home after a difficult interaction with a parishioner, wondering why I kept trying. It has been said that Christians are the only "army" that shoot their own wounded. And sadly, I've seen that too.

Yet the fishbowl struggle is often a blessing. It keeps you vulnerable and humble. However, it is also the scariest part of the job. Your actions have the potential to break the very thing you love and have worked so hard to build. That in itself causes a deep anxiety most folks outside of the fishbowl cannot understand.

We're all prone to screw-ups, but getting to the place where we can fail without viewing ourselves as a fail ure is key. Unfortunately, that only happens one mistake at a time. We have to learn to own up to our mistakes and then continue to move forward. I had to face my failures early in recovery. I had to cut off every temptation to identify who I am by what I have done wrong.

When we fail, we don't have to unpack and live there, obsessing over our inadequacy. We acknowledge what has happened, own our mistakes, apologize when necessary, and keep moving. No one is perfect.

Brene' Brown[8] would say we fear not being enough. I fear both that I can't offer hope to enough people, and that my honesty will sacrifice the hope I'm offering. Multiple times on a Sunday morning, people come to me and say "thank you" and begin to share portions of their story. There's no greater honor yet at the same time, I want to scream, "I am jacked up! I have more issues than you! It's just a blog! I have no idea what I am doing! I'm barely saved!"

**What shame whispers, I want to shout.**

The power of vulnerability is life-changing. We can have really good days, and their joys are very real. But even in our best moments, struggles leave anyone in the fishbowl feeling fragile and, often, alone. All it takes is one negative word, one trigger, to send us spiraling again, drowning in the very thing we so carefully and lovingly created.

No matter how successful you may be, all of us struggle. On my best day, anxiety still has the chance to kick my butt. If I said anything different, I would be lying. The spotlight doesn't erase struggles. And really, isn't that a great relief? Even Jesus in the Garden of Gethsemane shed literal drops of blood. Even our Savior, in his most significant hour, struggled under the pressure, **feeling crushed like an olive into oil.**

But you aren't Jesus. Nothing matters more than you–who you are at your core–apart from your title, success, brand, organization, ministry, or any other ways you have devoted your energy. No matter how much you seem to have your shit together, everyone needs a Savior.

In therapy, I learned shame is best fought when I share my pain and am met with compassion. God doesn't define me by my failures, but he speaks to me with kindness. He deals with me patiently. God calls me his child. No matter what I have done, I am worthy of his love.

**Self-Care Reflections:**

You've almost completed two weeks of self-care journaling! We've looked at a lot of hard things and failures, so let's switch gears. What is one positive thing you have noticed about yourself since we started?

_____
_____
_____
_____
_____
_____
_____

What is one thing you need to hear when you mess up? Write it down so you have it when that failure comes.

_____
_____
_____
_____
_____
_____

What does owning up and moving forward look like for you? (Hint: it doesn't include continually rehearsing your failures.) Commit now to taking those steps, so you're ready when failure comes.

_____
_____
_____
_____
_____
_____

## Messy Grace Mantra:

Healing is a process that includes relapse. I will get up again because I know healing is worth experiencing. I will have a plan when relapse happens.

# DAY 13: SAVING A LIFE REQUIRES MORE THAN TIDYING UP.

I was abused as a preschooler. I can see the pink crepe myrtle behind us in the side yard. I can hear the sound of a table saw, where my dad was building on the other side of the house. I can feel the stickiness of the Alabama evening air. And the smell of a sweaty teenage boy makes me cringe to this day. Those impressions have been burned into my psyche and can never be erased.

At times it seems like that is what everyone else wanted to do: erase it. Sweep the incident under the rug and move forward. But I was not afforded that luxury. They probably thought I was so young that I wouldn't even remember it. But the truth is, I have been remembering it every day for the past thirty years.

In the wake of a disaster, it's normal to send in a clean-up crew. But search and rescue has to happen first, and even cleaning up is just one piece of the long-term strategies to rebuild.

Unfortunately, for a long time, I too tried to pretend it didn't happen. And I fell into the patterns of addiction, mental illness, and self-destructive coping skills.

When I first starting having flashbacks, I tried to reason with myself. "He only took my innocence," I'd say. *Only.* That's one heck of a word. It was only a loss of childhood. A loss of comfort. *Only* applies to one-day sales at your favorite store. *Only* cheapens a thing. It was not *only* anything.

Yet my innocence was replaced with insecurity. All of my life, I felt I was never good enough.

Never man enough.

Never loved enough.

I was certain that my fragile nature was an inconvenience.

But at some point, you have to ask yourself, what if the very things that have destroyed you can lead you toward peace? What if the answer is not diminishing our experience or trying to ignore it, but leaning into them? What if the only way toward healing is to first acknowledge what has happened? To say, I am different. But I am not less.

There will be times when you will want to just pick up and move on. You will be tempted to pack your secrets back into the recesses of your soul because you feel like such a mess and everyone else seems so clean. You don't want to open the closets and let the skeletons out, to unearth the harsh words, the deep wounds, the abandonment, the lessons not learned.

But you have to remember this is a process. In the words of Kate Pieper, LMFT, recovery is a marathon, not a sprint. I was molested at the age of three, but I did not begin to actively deal with the repercussions of that trauma until twenty-six years later. I've learned that in the wake of total disaster, running away is futile. It's better to seek refuge, not just escape. Seek help. And as crazy as it sounds, just stand still and get better.

**Self-Care Reflections:**

> If you've spent a while (weeks, months, years) running, what are some of the realities you running from?

_____

_____

_____

_____

_____

_____

_____

Now that you've listed your realities, do you have someone safe to share them with? Someone helpful and supportive? Who is it? If not, Google therapists or counselors in your area today. Make a phone call. Make an appointment. Take care of yourself. You deserve it.

---
---
---
---
---
---
---

If you have never told someone your story, and the thought of it is overwhelming, maybe you could start by writing it down. Pen and paper are some of the greatest medicine known to man. Write it like you're writing a letter to the one person in life you trust the most. From there, you can hide it, burn it, or share it. But at least you will have faced it.

---
---
---
---
---
---
---

## Messy Grace Mantra:

I will not deny my reality. I will learn to walk openly and honestly with God and people I can trust.

# DAY 14: IN THE MIDST OF ANXIETY, I WILL CONTINUE TO LOOK FOR BEAUTY & GOODNESS.

Anxiety is so hard to describe to those who have never experienced it. For days at a time, I'll have a gnawing sensation in my stomach. I constantly check the rearview mirror when I drive, looking for a would-be wreck, or a cop. And often, I wish life came with a rearview mirror. The uneasy feeling only goes away when I sleep, but even sleep is light and fitful.

At one time, every time I felt anxious, I would question my faith. *Had I not prayed enough? Should I read another chapter of the Bible? I did tithe last week and two weeks before that, right? So why did I feel so off?* Some of my old thinking still crops up during anxious times, and I assume God is checking over my shoulder, too. But every time, I draw a blank.

The truth is, anxiety doesn't care if you've been good or not. It's going to torment you regardless. Anxiety doesn't only hit on the side of the road. Sometimes it strikes during happy hour with your friends or at the exact moment your co-workers are laughing at an apparently hilarious joke. Anxiety is crying in your car after dropping off the kids at school or knowing what it feels like to cry in the shower so no one hears your sobs.

As an extrovert, anxiety is the one thing that causes me to hide, silent and isolated. Yet even at my worst, I sometimes find myself pretending to care about the struggles of the whole damn world as long as I can remain anonymous in my own suffering. It means there are times I smile at a friend, wishing they knew I was dying on the inside, and equally thankful they are unaware.

But I have introverted friends who don't have this same experience with anxiety at all. They would never think to invite someone into their suffering. They have to be intentional about staying in touch with others when they are not well, because withdrawing into one's own head is just their natural inclination. Either way, living with anxiety is stressful. People who know your diagnosis ask how you're doing. How do you begin to answer that question? How do you adequately explain something you don't even understand yourself? It's exhausting fighting with your own head. This is why it is important to surround yourself with people who will love you fiercely and sit with you in times of struggle, while still calling "bullshit" on irrational thoughts. In the words of Kate Pieper, LMFT, "You're in your head without adult supervision."

A friend of mine once said, "Anxiety is not your Grandma's kind of worry."[9] It does not care if you have faith or not. In fact, my experience with anxiety is even *more* tumultuous when I question it from a Christian perspective. I try to be faithful, to do all the right things. But I still walk around with tightness enveloping my throat. Scripture promises a garment of praise for a spirit of heaviness. There are times I think, "I'd like to cash in that particular promise right about now."[9]

But I also know that **God isn't anxious** . He's not caught off guard by unforeseen events, and He certainly isn't nervously checking my performance against a task list to see if He can take care of me or not. He's constant. His faithfulness teaches me to stay faithful, even when my hands shake for no reason. Anxiety doesn't make sense. It may still creep up my spine and whisper white noise in my ears tomorrow, but I'll also have another chance to see more of beauty and good, too. Because God is constant and faithful, I'll have a new day and new chance to be faithful, too.

My worst days take me back to my second day in ICU, waiting to see if my liver would recover. In that moment, there was not an ounce of performance or pretense available to me. All I had was my mess. Yet in the midst of my brokenness, I heard God's voice like a gentle, soothing whisper. He didn't shout. He wasn't pushy or overbearing. He just stayed, providing a calm in the midst of my storm-tossed life, and reassured me, *"I'm not finished with you yet."* This was the strongest version of God I've ever experienced. It was a defining moment in my life. I'll never forget it.

Sometimes we feel lost, stuck, frustrated, or disconnected. Sometimes we feel like our stories don't matter. Sometimes I think I've written all there is for me to write and I might as well find a new hobby. But in that ICU room, I realized my hard days don't define me. Panic attacks suck, but they don't last forever.

**Self-Care Reflections:**

Maybe you don't struggle with anxiety, but we have all experienced hard times. In the midst of really tough days, have you ever been surprised by peace that overwhelms you? If so, what was that experience like?

_____

_____

_____

_____

_____

_____

_____

I believe none of our stories are over yet. If so, what do you want the next chapter of your life to look like?

_____

_____

_____

_____

_____

_____

_____

When anxiety strikes, whether it's a panic attack or just an extremely anxious day, I need reminders that they don't last forever. What's something you can write down right now that you need to remember the next time anxiety hits?

_____

_____

_____

_____

_____

_____

_____

## Messy Grace Mantra:

I choose to believe God is not finished with me, and the feelings of anxiety will pass.

# DAY 15: I WILL LET GO OF WHAT LIFE SHOULD BE LIKE. INSTEAD, I WILL ACCEPT CIRCUMSTANCES AS THEY ARE.

Acceptance is *hard*. People talk about mindfulness and being present in the moment, but when really bad days show up, it is really hard to be in them. In the past, I would vent, shout and cry, but failed to seek practical steps to work through my problems. I would try to run from my circumstances and blame others for my mistakes.

After my suicide attempt, I discovered that sometimes in order to deal with the problem, I first need to feel better. I learned when emotions go up, rational thinking goes down. Focusing on the "now" means figuring out how to deal with my current symptoms before tackling the roots of longstanding issues.

I also need a safe space to work through my problems, a place where my emotions are protected and respected. Five minutes after someone hurts me or an external stimulus triggers an internal response may not be the best time to work through feelings. I may need a little time and space to breathe and feel better. Accepting my emotions allows them to come down and my rational thinking to increase. It's often the smartest move I can make. Once that happens, I can then work through the issue.

We all mess up: some of us more than others. Some of us make mistakes that seem "bigger" than others, but we all make mistakes. We can't blame the choices we make on family history or former friends or employers or the government or God. We have to own our mistakes and the fact that they affect other people. We all make decisions and sometimes we just make the wrong ones. We often miss the current step of our recovery, by digging past it, to the roots, becoming obsessed with things it isn't time to heal yet. Focus on what you can deal with today. Instead of trying to get from point A to point Z, just take the next step in front of you. Go from A to B. It's all you have to do.

The best thing any of us can do is focus on today and the people who love us, those who push us to be our best and love us even at our worst. We can't run from our present circumstances, so we might as well lean into them, name our pain, and let God's grace wash over us, as we intentionally work through our current situation. Focus on the now. We'll get to the next soon enough.

**Self-Care Reflections:**

As Kate Pieper, LMFT, says, "Sometimes anxiety makes us forget where we are and that we're safe." Reminding yourself that you're in the now is called grounding. Kate suggests noting the date, day and time when rough moments happen. Place your feet flat on the floor and remind yourself this is NOW."

_____
_____
_____
_____
_____
_____

Do you have a calm space, somewhere your emotions are protected and respected? Who loves you at your best and your worst? How often do you spend time with those people?

_____
_____
_____
_____
_____
_____

On particularly hard days, are there places or people you should avoid? List them here and give yourself permission to distance yourself on these days.

_____
_____
_____
_____
_____
_____
_____

## Messy Grace Mantra:

I choose to live in this moment. This is NOW. And I am grateful for NOW.

# DAY 16: I GET TO CHOOSE WHO I LET INTO MY DEEP SPACES.

As I lay in the ICU bed, still not completely sure I wanted to keep living, my wife encouraged me to call my parents. I was physically weak, emotionally exhausted, scared of what the future might hold, and humiliated. My wife hoped talking to my mom would be the comfort I needed and the push to keep going.

But that didn't happen. My parents didn't come to the ICU, or to psych ward that followed. It didn't matter that I had been a great kid, given them virtually no trouble all my life, been a star student, and busted my ass to make them proud. They certainly weren't proud of me in this moment, as I lay in a crumpled pile, wishing I had died. It's one of the most painful memories of my life.

Four years after my attempt, I have two children who adore my parents. Even though Mom and Dad's absence at a critical moment cut deep, I believe in the power of second chances and I want to believe they have learned from their hurtful response.

So what do you do with the people in your life you can't easily push away? Those who are permanent fixtures, those whom have both hurt you and been hurt by you? In my life, the answer to that question looks like checking in with them on my terms. I set the pace of our relationship now. Because they chose not to be a part of my support system when I needed them most, they don't get to be always "in the know" that I am whole.

I respectfully let my parents know how I am doing, but I don't divulge any personal details that make me uncomfortable. My dad and I never discuss my mental health. And I can't talk to my mom about my anxiety because it always ends with a prayer and text messages of random verses from the Bible. I know it's how she best knows to deal with things, but in the moment, it does nothing but frustrate me further.

I have to remind myself they aren't at the same place as me, and don't have the same resources I do. It is perfectly okay to say, "Thanks for asking, but I am not willing to talk about this with you."

You also do not have to be a doormat. This is especially important for people of faith, who have been taught that turning the other cheek means standing around waiting to be smacked. You can absolutely walk away from a toxic person for the sake of your own mental, emotional, and spiritual health.

I've learned that forgiving someone doesn't mean you have to continue to be as close as you once were. Even if you choose to maintain a relationship, you have the right to set new boundaries. You don't have to be deeply connected to people who don't support you. Surround yourself with people who are in your corner and believe in you.

**Self-Care Reflections:**

> You get to choose who you let into your deep spaces. You don't have to sacrifice your truth or violate your recovery or boundaries in order to make someone else feel better. Is there someone you still want in your life, but with whom you need to create new boundaries? Who is it? If so, what would new boundaries look like?

If you aren't sure who you've allowed into the deep places of your heart, it may help to create a list. Who are the who people have permission to know your frustrations and struggles? Who are the people who don't? The healthiest people have "inner-circle people" and "outer-circle people".

_____

_____

_____

_____

_____

_____

_____

## Messy Grace Mantra:

I will give myself permission to have an inner circle based on the quality of my relationships.

# DAY 17: IF ADDICTION IS DROWNING, RECOVERY IS A LIFE RAFT.

---

For the person who longs for freedom, the cycle of addiction is exhausting. We swim and kick, pushing against the waters that look so playful from the shore, but we wonder if we're going to drown. Trying to live a pure life, wholeheartedly devoted to our spouse and our faith is like swimming against the tide of culture that believes pornography is "no big deal."

If it's no big deal, why is it so hard to escape?

Even after months of hard, hard work, in one moment of exhaustion I can still easily give up the fight and let the tide of addiction carry me back. It's amazing to me how easy it is, still, to just give up. But each time I do, I'm tossed and tumbled against sand that scrapes away scabs. Broken shells and broken promises cut deep, and the cycle continues another day.

Even when we break free, freedom feels so fragile. My addiction often speaks lies that sound like this, "You're free. For now." I'm not sure I have ever believed that I could truly be permanently free. Listening to that lie fills me with shame and discouragement. The only way I have found to work through my addiction is to walk away, fill my mind with good things, and embrace the intimacy of God.

Each time I intentionally choose intimacy with my wife over the perversion of pornography, God's comforting and empowering grace washes away more of my shame. And when I mess up, being honest and accountable to someone I trust becomes a buoy. In the middle of a raging sea, real relationships – with God, with my wife, with my friends - save me.

Maybe for you it's not pornography. It could be drugs or alcohol, food, shopping, or social media, or any number of things. No one has a perfect life, but mine is proof that no matter how hard it gets, no matter how much we feel like outcasts, there is always a path forward. Recovery is often like a winding river, unlike anything you could imagine. But recovery is worth it. Self-care is part of that battle, but it's also what enables us to keep swimming.

**Self-Care Reflections:**

It has been said that confession is good for the soul. Do you have someone, such as a trusted friend, a family member, or a professional to whom you confess your struggles?

_____
_____
_____
_____
_____
_____
_____

What is one way you can encourage yourself today? Is it a good book? A fight song? A Bible verse that lifts you up?

_____
_____
_____
_____
_____
_____
_____

Grace is one way we fight the current that would love to see us drowned. Grace feels a lot like forgiveness but it also feels like the power to begin living a better life. What is one way you can show yourself grace today?

---
---
---
---
---
---
---
---

## Messy Grace Mantra:

I will celebrate the victories and progress I have had. I will continue to be honest and accountable with my support system, as well as give myself grace while I persevere.

# DAY 18: I WILL FIND MY REASON FOR GETTING OUT OF BED EACH MORNING.

As a teen and throughout my 20s, I considered pursuing everything from religion to military service. I wasn't sure what I was supposed to do with my life, but I was certain it would be magnificent. I was sure it would involve stages and possibly fame. I was accustomed to excelling, and didn't God promise me a hope and a future?

My hope and future look much different than I had thought. God does have a magnificent plan for me, but He isn't only impressed if I preach to an audience of 10,000. He cares just as much about my commitment to my wife and children.

I used to talk a lot about God's glorious promises of a hope and a future. But now I find that hope and future in the mornings, when I have the honor of fixing our children breakfast while my wife has a few extra minutes to "become human" on the couch. Our marriage nearly fell apart due to my constant busyness and drive to do something big. But God's grace is greater than even our biggest mistakes. Now, I have the privilege of making her coffee and helping with household chores.

I see now that the "small things" in my day are really the big things of life. The "small things" are moments with my family. I have always loved my family, but instead of viewing them as a job, I now realize they are my greatest gifts.

I find my hope in the fact that God connects with me on a personal level, not because of my great ability, but because of the fact that God values who we are above what we do. He values me as His son, in the same way that I cherish my wife and children because they are mine.

When I take my last breath on earth, I won't be thinking of crowds or website stats. I pray to God I won't be thinking of failures or any sort of disappointment I ever faced, but instead of all the "small things". The time I took to breathe. To kiss my son on the forehead. To reach across the kitchen table and hold my wife's hand. To notice the way my daughter smells behind the ears. These tiny moments are the ones that matter the most to me now. This is the reason I get out of bed in the morning, and I'm choosing to do this with all of my heart.

**Self-Care Reflections:**

What are you most thankful for? What gifts do you see in your life right now, both large and small?

_____

_____

_____

_____

_____

_____

How do you see the concept of self-care changing your priorities?

_____

_____

_____

_____

_____

_____

We're nearing the end of this self-care journal. Are there things you are doing differently for yourself as a result of this process? List them here.

_____

_____

_____

_____

_____

_____

_____

## Messy Grace Mantra:

I will focus on the small joys of each moment. I will remember to celebrate the small successes in life, even while I wait for the big things to happen.

# DAY 19: I WILL RESPECT MY LIMITS, & FOCUS ONLY ON THINGS THAT MAKE ME BETTER.

As a person with mental illness, there is so much I can't control, like a panic attack in the middle of the work day, or waking up to the fog of depression on a beautiful summer Saturday morning. But I can always control how I take care of myself. I can respect my limits, fight distraction, and focus on recovery.

Before my suicide attempt, I was addicted to connection. Phone, text, email, social media, blogging, radio: you name it, I was there. I had no clue what boundaries were or how they applied to my life. But on the psych ward, I couldn't have my cell phone and had specific times I could call my approved "safe people." I was only allowed to engage with my support system during those days. The policy helped me reconnect with my true self.

I used to think I needed to be 100% accessible 100% of the time. Because I had no boundaries, the ever-present busyness kept me from the people who matter most. I was a "yes man" to any person or project I thought would make me feel important. A friend once called me an "attention whore," and sadly, he was right.

After my suicide attempt, I accepted my limitations and my need to say "no." I have learned that boundaries protect us and point us toward the people and things that truly matter. Now, I decline more projects than I accept. I have learned to choose only activities that add value to my life, my marriage, or my family. I have learned to say no. And I'm happier than I have ever been.

After setting healthy boundaries, I needed to learn to respect my limits physically. This includes things like uninterrupted sleep, good nutrition, unstructured time, and time with my family and friends.

Self-care means not staying up all hours of the night to binge on my favorite show or read just one more chapter. I find when I'm tired, my symptoms are worse.

I've also learned to practice better eating. Instead of making excuses for why I can't make healthier choices, I take my nutrition seriously. I don't skip meals anymore, as low blood sugar intensifies anxiety. I have found that my productivity at work has increased and my overall mood and sense of well-being is much better. Now I eat with the goal of getting the most out of my day.

**It's hard to take care of myself, to acknowledge my limits and make my health a priority, but it's worth the fight.** I'm fighting for the people I love. And I'm fighting against whatever tries to pull my focus on anything that doesn't support me and make me better.

Fight for your own life. Because **life is worth living.**

**Self-Care Reflections:**

> If you could unplug for an hour, what would you do for yourself? Try it today and find out!

_____

_____

_____

_____

_____

_____

_____

How many hours do you typically sleep a night? What do you normally eat in a day? Don't know? Why not keep a sleep journal or a food journal this week? 6-7 hours of sleep is a minimum for the average adult. And if you write down everything you put in your body during one day, for an entire week, you might be surprised at what you will learn.

Do you practice a nonreligious Sabbath? Giving yourself 24 hours as a rest from working is something trainers and personal coaches often recommend. Try to set aside a day where the majority of "work" is not taking place. Report back in with yourself after a month of practicing this new habit.

## Messy Grace Mantra:

I am growing and learning. I can disconnect for a time without fear. Those who love me will wait for me and will respect my need to quiet my mind.

# DAY 20: I DON'T HAVE TO LIVE INSIDE THE IDENTITY OF A PERSON WHO WAS WRONGED FOREVER.

When I was twelve, I fell off my bike and hurt my arm, bad. We didn't have much money and my dad, an EMT, was from a different generation. You didn't go to the hospital every time you took a tumble. He wanted to ice it and keep an eye on it. "Probably just a bad fall, bud. Take a couple of Tylenol." He wasn't being a jerk. He was just calm under pressure, and very practical. While all of that makes sense now, back then, it did not.

The next day, when it still hurt, we went for x-rays. "He has a hairline fracture," the doctor said, pointing to the flimsy film. A few weeks with a cast, names and faces in Sharpie marker, and I could officially say I'd had broken a bone. It was the manliest thing I'd ever done.

My dad was in the driveway when the pea gravel fooled my bike's tire. He knew I was hurt, even if he didn't know to what extent, and he did what he thought was right. It didn't soften the blow, my arm was still broken, but what if I had taken a baseball bat to his truck in a fit of rage because he didn't respond in the way I felt most appropriate? What if, upon returning from the orthopedist, my Mom slapped him in the face for not immediately taking me to the ER?

That was my response to the Church for more than a decade. A baseball bat and a slap in the face. I'd been wronged by religion. In my brokenness, I was outraged. I had open sores left by my experiences. Instead of allowing the Shepherd of my soul to heal me, I smeared my pain on the Church's steeple and dared it to question my response.

A few years ago, my wife and I supported a family trying to start a new Church. Several couples met in our home, determined to be different. Only, we were worse than the places we had left.

For weeks, we wallowed in our weariness and confessed all the ways we'd been harmed by religion. Eventually, we left that angry little group. You can't find healing when all you do is pick at your scabs.

After ten years, I have begun to meditate over past hurts and consider my most faithful response to the Church today. But why did it take me ten years to get to this point? We waste so much energy with all of the thoughts and role-playing we do in our heads before we try and find a solution. I did it for way too long.

Nearly two months ago, I secretly drove over to my childhood home, a tiny house in rural Alabama. I stood next to the pink crepe myrtle in the side yard without any words. None were needed. Thirty years before, I had lost my innocence to the selfishness of a neighbor in that very spot. For years, I looked back on the days and weeks that followed my childhood sexual abuse with anger. I felt that not nearly enough was done to help me. There was no counseling or prosecution. My parents did what they thought was right, but some wounds require more than prayer and turning the other cheek.

I broke that day in the side yard. I broke because of an injustice like those that occur in too many congregations by too many people who should know better. I broke like so many of God's people do. I'm thankful to have closed the door on that victimhood. Bad things happened, but I don't have to live inside the identity of a person who was wronged forever.

That day I shed my tears, got back in the car, and drove away from the scene of that long-ago crime. It takes time to get to the place where we can accept that moving forward is not saying nothing bad happened. Yes, what happened was wrong. But setting up camp and dwelling on these wrongs only compounds the problem. I have decided I want to live as one who acknowledges the pain of being done wrong, who has the courage to return and call my pain what it was, and then can pick up and move on.

I am thankful that grace extends to all of us. I want to be defined by more than the kid who was once broken in the side yard.

**Self-Care Reflections:**

Moving forward doesn't mean you invalidate past hurts. It means you are beginning to own your experiences instead of allowing them to own you. Today, write down one old hurt you are ready to let go.

_____
_____
_____
_____
_____
_____
_____

What is one concrete way you can move forward today? Is it a conversation with someone who has hurt you? Is it confessing your mess to someone you hurt in order to reconcile a relationship?

_____
_____
_____
_____
_____
_____
_____

Words are important. How you refer to yourself matters. Do your refer to yourself as a victim, a survivor, or a thriver? What do you need in order to call yourself a "recovery thriver"?

_____

_____

_____

_____

_____

_____

_____

## Messy Grace Mantra:

I will start taking steps toward grieving, accepting, and forgiving myself, the Church, and others for injuring me. I will not push myself in this process, but will give myself grace as I learn how to live without vengeance.

# DAY 21: I WILL BE PATIENT & KIND WITH MYSELF THROUGH THE LONG-TERM PROCESS OF RECOVERY.

A note from Kate: *Remember, this is a marathon journey. We are running the race and laying aside all the shit that gets in the way. Be patient with yourself through this entire process. Eventually, you will figure out why you are still alive, but honestly, that could take four or five years or so. The time it will take for true healing is just one more reason why you cannot go through recovery alone. We all need encouragement when we lose our way.*

Once you start to feel better, you can answer the next important question: What is my life all about? Figure out what on earth you're doing here...and then do *that* with all your heart. If you don't know that answer yet, ask. Ask God, ask a friend who knows God. Find a therapist or get alone and get quiet and figure out what it is that makes your heart beat.

Learning to value your own mental, physical, spiritual, and emotional health leads you that much further down the road toward wholeness.

You're a survivor! You can do what feels impossible! You can respect the recovery process by no longer picking at your scabs. You're still here! Still standing. Hurt? Sure. Alive? No doubt. Able to the hard work to find healing? Hell yes.

**Self-Care Reflections:**

> What are three things you've learned through this self-care journey? How will you apply them to your life moving forward?

_____

_____

_____

_____

_____

_____

_____

Have you found a community where you can tell your story? Is it a recovery group? A church group? A small group of friends?

_____

_____

_____

_____

_____

_____

Have you joined our virtual community of recovery rockstars? The Grace is Messy Facebook Group is a place for messy people to come together and support one another.

_____

_____

_____

_____

_____

_____

## Messy Grace Mantra:
I will continue forward and not be afraid to live!!

# RESOURCES

My book, *From Pastor to Psych Ward: Recovery from a Suicide Attempt is Possible* is a collection of essays that chronicle the events leading up to my suicide attempt, and how I found healing from it all. If you know anyone who has experienced abused, been addicted, or lives with any myriad of mental health issues, my story will offer them hope and a chance to say, "me too".

At iamsteveaustin.com, I have an exclusive member library, full of great content. From downloadable, printable manifestos to iPhone wallpapers, and more. Best of all? **It's free!**
Sign up for my newsletter and get the freebies today!

Are you looking for a crisis coach? I'd love to recommend my peer and personal friend, Faydra Koenig. As *America's Crisis Coach,* Faydra is changing lives by offering practical and powerful ways to overcome tragedy.
Check out her site at doinglifewithfaydra.com

TheMighty.com has incredible resources and stories of tragedy and triumph. I have been privileged to write for Mental Health on The Mighty on several occasions.

If you're looking for a book specifically about the journey to recovery after a loved one commits suicide, check out J.J. Landis's memoir, *Some Things You Keep*[10].

If you'd like to learn how to craft your story in a way that encourages others and connects with people in a deep and powerful way, *The Writer's Toolkit* (e-book and e-course) is the perfect place to start. Check out iamsteveaustin.com/shop for more info!

# BIBLIOGRAPHY

Steve Austin, From Pastor to a Psych Ward: Recovery from a Suicide Attempt Is Possible, 1st ed. (Birmingham, Alabama: Steve Austin, 2016).

Steve Austin, The Writer's Toolkit: How to Own and Craft Your Story, 1st ed. (Birmingham, Alabama: Steve Austin, 2016).

"What Is Self-Care?" UKY Student Affairs Center. Accessed July 01, 2016. https://www.uky.edu/StudentAffairs/VIPCenter/downloads/self care defined.pdf.

"Braver Living and Loving." COURAGEworks. Accessed July 01, 2016. http://www.courageworks.com/.

Brennan Manning, Lion and Lamb: The Relentless Tenderness of Jesus, (Fleming H Revell Co, 1986).

Brown, Brené. "Brené Brown." TED: Ideas worth Spreading. Accessed June/July, 2016. http://www.ted.com/speakers/brene_brown.

Brown, Brene' "Dr. Brene Brown: "Shame Is Lethal" - SuperSoul. tv." SuperSoultv. Accessed September 01, 2016.http://www.supersoul.tv/supersoul-sunday/dr-brene-brown-shame-is-lethal.

Brown, Brené. Rising Strong. Random House, 2015.

Austin, Steve. "Anxiety: Not Your Grandma's Kind of Worry." Grace Is Messy. Accessed September 01, 2016. http://www.patheos.com/blogs/graceismessy/2013/10/22/6998/.

Landis, JJ, Some Things You Keep: Letting Go, Holding On, Growing Up. (JJ Landis, 2015).

51977918R00053

Made in the USA
Middletown, DE
15 November 2017